Health Carefully

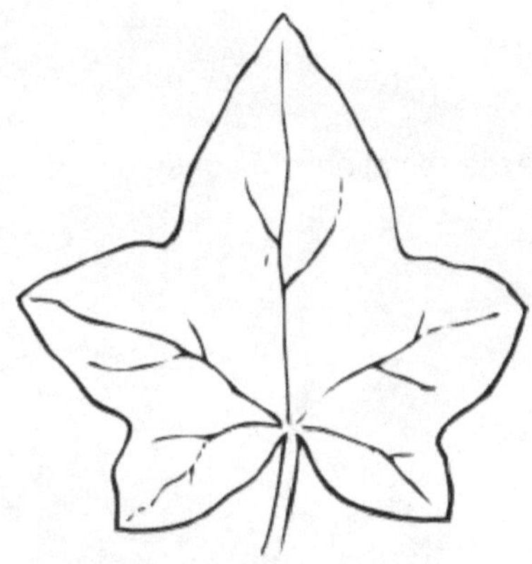

Jesse Tsinajinnie Maloney

Dedications

This work is dedicated to my wife, Julie Maloney. I love you more, more & more, I love you 'til my heart gets sore.

Acknowledgements

I'd like to thank poets Pamela Uschuk and William Pitt Root. I'd also like to thank my mother, Joan Dulan, and my sister, Violet Skinner. And special thanks to Dr. Karunesh Kumar Agrawal and the Taj Mahal Review.

Notes

Patient Appeared in 'Images Magazine' 2011

Desert Weed Appeared in 'Turtle Island Quarterly' Winter/Spring 2016

The Time Traveler Appeared in 'Peach Velvet Mag: Issue 2' Summer 2018

Last Lap Appeared in 'The Taj Mahal Review: Vol. 17 Number 2' December 2018

Winter's God Appeared in 'About Place' May 2019

Contents

Chapter 1

Tuba City

Winter's God

I.

Winter's God, blow your nose on my rooftop like a glonnie shivering on the third day of

withdrawal, begging through sneezes for white man's change.

Tear my lungs out and use them as your handkerchief. Stuff them back in my chest trailing shimmering white snot with Rhyolite blood fault lines across my throat.

II.

Winter's God, caress imaginations of babes with red and evergreen ribbons on street lights ballooning translucent golden halos against your nightly dandruff flakes.

Advent calendars are marked with tiny fingers and hymns sung with tiny voices in your honor countdown the stillbirth of your offspring, miscarried, misunderstood and exalted nonetheless.

III.

Winter's God, indiscriminately strangle pipes until they crack and secrete into aquifers and Sioux burial grounds in South Dakota. Their weak craftsmanship and reasons for being are none of your concern.

Mass casualties occurred in your breasts and we wonder if you shed tears of ice as women and children were forced to walk long with muskets pointed at them as they fell starved and frozen in your embrace.

IV.

Winter's God, you're frail this year, barely mustering the strength to cover the highest peaks, your frost is thin and quickly fades leaving little trace of once raucous town closing tirades.

We are destroying you but it's anything but personal, no more personal than silly ambitious corpses left as landmarks on your majesty's Everest, green boots, red boots, festive and dead.

V.

Winter's God, you are unhinged, unrestrained, indifferent, amoral but in the end, God. Should you perish by our hand, we murder our own design.

Winter's God, we tremble under your power and beg to continue to fear your wrath and fury. Let us suffer our sins against you, let us repent of trespasses against you with fall after fall, foot after foot of unrelenting blizzard from October to March, from Winslow to the Blackhills, let us huddle in small corners in insignificant dwellings, allow us the privilege to feel awed, humble, and enveloped in the mercy of the season.

Cries of the Southwest

From a distance it's easy
to be enthralled
by the bazaars and annual
Tuba City fair.

 The sight of traditional Hopi dancers
in full butterfly dress impress
even the most travel worn
tourists trekking Route 66.

However, there are spaces
 between ceremonies and
 sunlight
that aren't accessible to
visitors.

They exist in the mundane,
in the hospital waiting rooms,
lines at the Basha's grocery
and the post office parking lot
 after hours.

From a distance
you
can see the Southwest's
heart in all of its beauty.

Over time you'll hear
its
 steady beat.

But I hear
its murmurs,
its palpitations,
its cries.

Desert Weed

Not enough rain is bad news for seed germination.
It creates an unpleasant climate. Too much rain, the
seed risks being washed away completely. It'll never
get the chance to bloom. And if the rain comes too

early or too late in the season then the whole opportunity to grow
in the first place is missed. A flower's a twenty something year
old floozy on a barstool. Space the drinks with care. What's
this evening's weather forecast?   Pleasantly plastered with a
70 percent chance of fucking. A flower's a floozy. A weed's a rapist.

Bull thorns, bull thorns, bull thorns stuck to my boots and tracked
in the house.
The wife neighs "My foot! My Foot!"
The wife neighs "What are these, thumbtacks?"
The wife neighs "My retarded husband!"
The wife neighs "Weed killer and the yellow hatchet!"
The wife neighs "Not later, now!"

I relace my boots, search for gloves and prepare for battle.
Yard work's a talent that's skipped my generation. Pulling,
chopping and collecting plants in black Hefty bags seems
 unnatural. If they grow and survive the elements, who's
to say they don't belong in our yard?
The wife neighs "Now!"

You're competitive, persistent, pernicious, insistent on
reaching that water well below the surface. And you don't
even reach it. You just reach for it. The result is blister

after blister from the handle of my pick axe. A bed of
desert weeds like the city of Prague at midnight is
three times as big underground. The techno music isn't
 coming from the bar above, it's from the dance club
 located below. And below that dance club is another
dance club. Five stories all below the earth Aryan DJ's
 spin different records at different times creating a muffled

rhythm-less sound like five pieces of assorted colored
bubblegum chewed until their sweetness is gone and
all that's left is a big bland blob of gray. The desert
weed like an unbearable synthesized beat pounding
from somewhere, I dig foot after foot never finding
its source. Hole after hole I create a proper burial
ground for pets. I could throw road kill in each one
and call it a day. But the weeds would pierce the
carcasses like they did our driveway.

A well-manicured lawn is a symbol of wealth and pride in
American culture. Obesity's a symbol of wealth and pride
in the Hawaiian culture. And beauty. I put away the rake
and axe. Accept natural laws of the barren land. What I
call noise, others might call music. When the wife sees a
weed I'll say the Navajos think of them as flowers.

They don't. But I'll say it anyway.

The Time Traveler

Tim Yazzie's his name.

He shuffled down
the Navajo side
of highway 160 West.
A quart of mint mouthwash in,
he did not feel the grille
of the rig lift him and
send him in flight
across three lanes
and a time zone.

His numb body skidded
and found its resting place
on the Hopi side
of highway 160 west.

Time of accident: November 8th 2006
8:01pm
Time of death: November 8th 2006
7:20pm

Yazzie's body
squared off by
four shades of yellow crime
scene tape,
each shade from a different roll
brought from a different precinct.

Officers in uniforms of
gray, blue, tan & brown
stare at clipboards
call superiors
mumble numbers into
walkie talkies.

Moons pass
Suns sets
and Yazzie's bones
now exposed
still rest in the center
of the square marked off
by plastic tape
surrounded by federal agents,
Navajo police, Hopi police
Arizona state troopers
and loved ones on the outskirts
filling out page after page of
paperwork.

Above ground burial
expedites travel
to the spirit world
three feet above earth.

Tim Yazzie's bones forever lie on
Hopi land
his body never moved
because no agreement
on jurisdiction
could be met.

A four way stalemate
like a game of chess played
with only kings for pieces
a bible's worth of paperwork
reads two non-contested details.

Time of accident: November 8th 2006
8:01pm
Time of death: November 8th 2006
7:20pm

Remember Tim Yazzie
and the rest.

Let the dead decompose above ground.

See them.

 Don't deny they walked among us.

All of us.

Working on the Rez

An ulcer burns my belly
jerking off
distracts the pain
cum hits the napkin
clear goo
dries in a yellowish crusty
stain
euphoric sensation fades
and replaced by my
hurt guts.

Work has me stressed
try not to medicate
too much.

Maybe a raise in pay
or a vacation
from impotent tasks
meaningless acts
paper work resulting in
notarized kindling
for the flame in my stomach.

stamped documents bearing
gold emblems
met with more disdain
than tanned soiled toilet tissue.

I should
challenge my king's authority
like Adam's sons of liberty
demand change, progress, purpose
something to boast and toast to
at the end of the week
instead of the need
to drown failures in ethanol and excuses.

The rush that'd come
from speaking out
pointing out
poisoned processes
and their antidotes
would feel almost as
good as
jerking off.

Substitute

The substitute teacher
is an abnormality woven
into the quilt of modern American
Education.

While the patterns of
principals, elderly crossing guards and
gym teachers are sewn in with
upholstery nylon holding cloth
firmly together with zig zag stitching at
the seams producing a blanket
capable of enveloping
providing warmth and comfort
for a children during formative
years, an unbreakable barrier
of plush cotton and pedagogy,
the substitute teacher is a
sheet of bottom shelf paper
towel threaded with flavorless
dental floss, tearing at
the slightest tug
 evaporating
under a warm sweat
the quilt of education
becomes a roll of
paper towels to be
thrown like a
football.

White Clay

Twelve thousand cans
a day. Twelve thousand
hisses and snaps,
a chorus of vacuum
packed gas escaping
singing into the night
and through the South
Dakota morning wobbling
legs, slurring voices,
belching noises, devolving
speech to grunts and
mutters, swerving wheels,
lightening wallets with chains
attached to jean belt loops so
they're not lost in
the transaction with every
hiss followed by the familiar
metal snap.

Chapter 2

Health Carefully

Last Lap

Her bare feet like
          empty sneakers   deflated
on crab grass   savoring earth
for the eightieth year.
Onion paper skin
        blisters under
                  hospital issued gown
          when we lock arms
   and walk the last lap
   in the garden marketed
to heal.
Eggshell picket fence
yield peeled paint
flakes like bits
 of snow on
dead azaleas.
          She walks
   without delusions
   of life beyond
life.
    She walks
  imagining below
     splitting
        fissures on Waiakea's giant
   chapped lips
careful not
  to step in lava.
   She walks
because it's doctor's   orders.

She walks
    because it's scheduled
clearly in dry erase pink
        cursive complemented
                    by pink hearts   on
            the whiteboard
    in the lobby.
    She walks
because   she
    can't run.

Ambulance with No Siren

No flashes, no wails, travelling five below
the speed limit, the ambulance's siren is
silent.

Inching through traffic, the imposing emergency
vehicle yields to pedestrians, slows at yellow lights
and stops at reds.

Designed to move like a 14,000 pound meteorite screaming at
all in its way, it's meant to hurl towards its
destination unrestrained by the rules of the road.

The tradeoff, the contract motorists enter accepts and
understands the necessary peril so that a service
may be implemented effectively with the hope that
in their moment of emergency, a path will be cleared
so that a savior may arrive swiftly.

But when the siren is silent and the rules of the road
are observed, hope is silent.

The siren blares life, the siren shrieks pain,
a pain that can still be felt and treated, a pain that
is not patient, a pain that cannot wait, a pain that
insists to be acknowledged by a siren responding
with equal earnest demanding to be heard.

A silent siren's destination is death.

Death is not an emergency.

Dust

Coral colored veins smoothed against
sand storms. Tubular branches
inhale full breaths of
dust.

sneeze blackened bits of blood
encapsulated in glistening mucus blobs in
violent rejection of unwanted foreign
bodies
riding
Southwest currents, bodies
touching mice
touching sage
touching Navajo
touching Hopi
touching youth
touching you
through
two
nostrils.

Admission
acceptance
welcoming foreign particles followed
by violent ejection
blasted back into Southwest
currents to drift and fondle
mice, sage, Navajo, Hopi
youth.

Hantavirus hides in
tool sheds, moist mouse
droppings coat screws and
allen wrenches. spiders
on webs drag dung
across rusty pliers into
concrete corners.
Southwest currents penetrate
damp spaces, invade
darkened corners, bathe
in rodent feces
migrating infected strands
inhaled through two
nostrils
irritating tubular branches.
Sneeze hardened blackened bits of
blood and
dust.

Nubs

Arteries hardened
and brittle
like glass pipes pumping
plasma, nutrients, oxygen
and too little
sugar to
hearts diseased clinging
precariously
to the first world.

Rotting toenails excite
orthopedists

Amputate just below the
knee so circulation
isn't kinked by
cracked glass pipes in the
calf and ankle.

300k salary takes
many many referrals
illegible signatures
days spent in waiting rooms
waiting to
partially die
under fluorescent parabolic
troffers.

chop, chop
Nubs
chop, chop
Crutches
chop, chop
Money
chop, chop
Yacht
chop, chop
Orgasm.

Patient

A 22 year old graduate of Northern Arizona University
is taken to the emergency room after his friends wrapped
a bleach soaked towel around the intoxicated
young man's head and sealed it with
duct tape around the neck with the
intent to give him a mild dopamine
release from the cleaning product fumes
but forgot about him for two hours
 because they were also
 intoxicated when concocting the idea.
                    His girlfriend in the experiment
                    playfully asks a nurse
                              "He's just gonna have
                              Headache right?"
        Whether he's a corpse or
        vegetable is discussed by
        doctors working triple shifts.
Florence Nightingale worked in dirtier
harsher conditions but death was welcome
over miracles that would leave the living
        lifeless.

An ultrasound turns a woman's insides
out making her broken heart the property
of Blue Shield.
        And then she goes to heaven on
        the rain cloud that soaks
        ambulances screeching
        into the parking lot.

        In the West the spirit is separate
from the body.
        In the East these are things that
are very real and concrete.

RN's always have a headache.
The NAU student is pronounced
dead and
room is made
for the next
        patient.

Your Shit

There are 17 distinct smells to shit
each one separating levels
of healthy and unhealthy
living.
(Suskind may disagree)
Hospital rooms lack fans
nurses gag
when your feces
stink of a hint of
bleach or
ammonia
on overly used
kitty litter boxes
kennels & cleaning product
Belvedere & Windex
or that mess
left early this A.M
in the commode
an 18th scent
the medical discovery
of our generation.

Elevator Music

Burger King Wrappers crinkle
among empty Shasta cans
under the fully accelerated gas pedal
of my parents' '73 copper Ford Pinto.

Mom's 22, two months overdue
overflowing in the passenger seat
No more fucking stops!
Red lights might as well be turquoise.
Dad roars into the military hospital parking lot
sprints to the emergency room entrance.

 he's turned away

They won't let us deliver here!
Dad runs somewhere else.
Mom reaches down her panties to
brush the hair on my
malleable little head
while I
squirm to get out of her.

A nineteen year old orderly approaches
the deathtrap with a gurney
fast.
Can you get out on your own ma'am?
Mom answers
No.

With the strength of ten struggling med students
he lifts her and readies her to be wheeled
in a military grade wheelchair.

Dad and doctor join him to push.

Delivery room's on the third floor.

Elevator doors open.

They enter.

Elevator doors close.

We ascend.

Elevator doors open
to show me
the hospital room
I was never born in

Chapter 3

Touch, Touch

Billy

October nights are colder your
breath chills me
at my knees I
guess I'm getting older
my gut grows with
every lost
evening
my tattoo's fading
more and more with
every friend that
leaves.

It's time to pour
out another drink.

You'll live on of
course you will in
memories and the lyrics
of countless songs
the ocean will sound
your name as it crashes
on imperfect snowflakes
softly landing on a sandy
beach
one day we will meet young
and thin like we used to
be on a white couch
sharing our
stories.

It's time to pour
out another drink.

Keep playing, keep playing
beautiful boy.

I can still hear you make
beautiful noise.

In the darkness my glass
is held up high
little stars like you
will light up the night so
bright I'll sleep through
every day and
curse God for taking
my friend
away.

Divorced

When water's not enough
When clean isn't
clean

pick at hangnails
and cracked, dry
palms

palms like desert
landscapes

When wine's not enough
When chocolate isn't
sweet

hangovers
 rosy cheeks with too many
lines to be dainty

now vomitus

irritate bellies

When cash's not enough
When a balanced spreadsheet
is just a spreadsheet

bedsheets tumble in
the dryer on Sunday evening

peak hours
to save money on

electricity

When fire's not enough
When scented candles
expire

drowned in their own
wax
melted
by unsupervised
neglected
flames

It is not time

It has been time
for quite

some time.

Catio

it takes three Dysons;
one for upstairs, one for
down and
one for the catio.
Sharks'll choke on
feline fur
strangling fan belts
clogging hoses.
Sharks'll choke and
die, only to be
left on the corner
Tuesday trash
day.

One vacuum cleaner
per
level, one litter
box per kittie,
four ounces of
gin per parent
shaken, chased with
white
grapefruit juice.

Sunlight hits the chicken
wired and mosquito
screened enclosure.

Shadows shift
gradually with
sunspots prompting
outstretched back
paws, toothy yawns
purring content.

Our catio, weather
proofed on a budget,
has a ping pong
table and
red lights so
our cats can
listen to metronomic
pops on paddles
over slurred commentary
under starlit
weeknights.

Bridesmaid

Dying corsages and a
mismatched mess
mosquitos nipping at
her lime green
dress
eleven o' clock the
knot was tied
the ceremony was
magical
I want to fuck some more
fill me with laughter
extra special brew
and cocaine
love me lustfully
these two nights.

A few hours of drunken
sleep and she wakes
with me
vodka in the morning
spinning dreams
around my heart
kisses upon kisses
before we
part
fill me with false hope
water by the liter
and Advil

love me lustfully
these two nights.

I'll work late
countdown the
drawer at the
video store
DVD rentals scratched
like my love
freeze during key
plot points
shaking awake critical
faculties
prohibit
suspending belief for
the sake of enjoyment.

This mismannered man is
missing she, Miho's music
makes me sing
fill me with laughter
extra special brew
and cocaine.

Cold Blood

My undying graciousness left inside your
room
I grasped your hands while inside
of you. It took three years to create
this hurt.

Three years of love to create the
pendulum that swung back and
crushed me.

I'll emerge from underneath it
eventually, I'll peer out
like a lizard in the desert
wiping my eyes with my
tongue
checking the weather
for subordinate clauses
and conditions
webbed hands now calloused
on hot sand.

Prince Albert

I pee sitting down sometimes
when my Prince Albert
goes missing
a penis without a Prince
Albert is just a penis
with two pee holes.

Normally I can twist
my dick clockwise and
seal the opening at the base of
the foreskin using gravity
and the ring as enough obstruction
to allow urine to flow through its
natural course and to its
destination;
toilet.

Without it, no matter
which way I twist it
I get
leakage
and splash on
my jeans and sleeves
from the first
hole.

In my late teens the
piercing allowed me to

expose myself without
fear of reprisals.

I wasn't flashing the young
ladies.

I was showing them a shiny
thing attached to
the end of my cock
as an icebreaker
not an assault
not a direct assault
but periphery degradation
an ancillary attack
to be forgotten until
a generation later
my name gains
recognition and my
philanthropy gains
traction
my face next to a
headline
cheeks plumper, hair
grayer, eyes softer but
they won't be mistaken
they'll remember
they'll all remember
and demand justice with
hashtags and an effective
 cyber campaign calling for
my end
fitting revenge for perverts
who didn't anticipate

the advent
of social media.

I'll respond to them:
I was young
I was dumb, I'm sorry
my father wasn't
around
but now I've a wife
three cats and when
I pee,
I pee
sitting
down.

Loved

Let the coffin shut
and seal what's left of
her
scent
in here
with me
and know
in my lives
I have loved.

Chapter 4

Questions Comments

Burns, Oregon

Count tattoos on
white supremacists
in Burns Oregon.

I count five crosses
on three men.

Some men have
two to balance
their forearms.

"You're asking too
many questions."

Count domestic
terrorists pardoned
inspiring more
terrorism.

I count two pardoned
by President Trump.

They're free to
terrorize in
Burns Oregon.

"You're asking too
many questions."

Count faces that
share a shade
like mine.

I count none during
my weekend visit.

I saw Mennonites
but didn't
see Utes.

"Stop asking so
many questions."

Three Haikus on Childhood PTSD

Cool

All my friends are cool

It's not really a good thing

They keep me lonely

Skull

Bulimic zombies

with salivating chompers

couldn't bite through this

Terror

I shiver alone

Skimming the surface of sleep

Scraping for a dream

Three Haikus on Why Haikus Don't Work in English

That That
He knew that *that* way
Was *way* away. English is
a stress based language.

Dit, Dash
Morse code's stressed with stress
On dits and dashes. Stress gives
Frequency meaning.

Japanese
Enough characters
In a syllabic language

No stress stress stress stressssssssssssssss'sss

Superman Versus the Polar Bears

He cannot fly.
He cannot wear a cape.
No laser blasts
from his eyes.

In a reality
where Superman fights giant
spiders and
polar bears
outside of his fortress of
solitude nullifying the
name
the bureaucratic win is
celebrated as quickly as
it is condemned as
tsunamis of
blame and shame crash
cracking
clavicles, scapulas and humeruses
but no spines because
there are no
spines to break.

After Watching Surviving R. Kelly on Lifetime

In the lore of Batman, Prince
is solidified
celebrated
Tim Burton's gift handled
with reverence for the
beloved source material
1989 the credits roll, the theme
fades and then the sexiest
baby making melody takes
over screeching *!Scandalous!*
originally, Michael Jackson was
to compose the slow songs
for the soundtrack
I believe the idea of those two
working together
Two kings heired to the same
throne
on the same album
is
better than the actual product
they'd produce.

In the lore of Batman, R Kelly
is a footnote, an
embarrassment to
Schumacher's
embarrassing franchise
ending flick

1995 the credits roll and
at some point R Kelly's
'Gotham City' plays
I don't know
maybe it doesn't
I never stuck around.

A $4.75 matinee against
the $7.50 full price ticket
stub I opted for the
evening performance
splurging on popcorn
7up and smuggled
mochi crunch.

Earlier, I exchanged
coins for cash
a dollar food stamp
equals ninety cents
cash
twelve stops on
the Leeward side of
the island for
nickel gum and I've
admission and
concessions
for Batman
Forever
in Pearl City.

Sparkle tells us to
listen to the lyrics
shoehorned into her comeback

the phrases 'me too' and 'time's up'
crooned over a public domain
string section mashed with
a tempo that sounds like
a straw blown in a milkshake
electronic vanilla bubbles go
bloopity bloop blup bloop
as they pop making a
milky mess of things.

Mr. Land's Bad Day

Why oh why'd Julie Horn's cleavage have to

make an appearance third hour? Teaching High School

American Government was already difficult enough for Mr. Land.

His shy awkwardness, his inability to teach with confidence,

his distrust in his words made it so difficult for him.

The words made sense in his head but the bored looks

they provoked from a room full of adolescents kept him

second guessing his next point. He paced slouched like a

confused gorilla staring at a chalk board filled with strange

symbols,

his back turned to his disappointed teenage audience.

He hadn't had sex in four months.

So you see, um, eh, the executive I mean the, uh, Judicial

Branch of-,

Mr. Land stopped.

All he could think of were Julie's perfect teenage titties, milky, ripe,

and stinking of a layer of pubescent sweat clashing with a splash

of Britney Spears' Curious. He wished he could be more like

Mr. Maloney over in English and pontificate loudly

captivating an audience, instilling wisdom on subjects he knew

absolutely nothing about.

Mr. Maloney could read the blurb on a book jacket and

come up with a semester's worth of material riddled with

his unique brand of bravado and bullshit. It was heroic.

"The judicial branch isn't... isn't... isn't necessarily the

most powerful of the two—I mean three—... Three?"

Mr. Land was losing them.

"You see the purpose of the Judicial Branch is to... to... um,"

Mr. land rubbed his sticky temple.

He felt his heart pick up a little speed. Blood coursed through

varicosity.

He should've studied special education in college.

He could've been teaching the retarded kids how

to read books on tape. It would've been easy, really fucking easy.

Instead, he was stuck with entitled sophomores.

One of them was Julie, slightly exposed, taunting Mr. Land

with a glimpse of her intermammary sulcus separating those

titties creating a little cavern into no man's land. She sat on

that God given ass. Goddamn that ass! He knew that, that ass

in particular, was better than any master's degree or doctorate.

A good shake and she'd be set for life.

His heart pumped blood beyond utilitarian appendages.

"Let me... just try to explain it this way,"

Mr. Land turned around.

      The students' expressions of boredom vanished with

      jaws hitting their desks, eyes as big as ping pong balls,

       the class was silent for a moment with a collective gasp

      suffocating the room.

Something was terribly wrong.

   "HE'S GOT A BONER!!!!!"

a boy in the front row cried.

    The class erupted with finger pointing and screams of

     "Oh, my God! Oh, my God! Oh my God!"

    Hands fumbled with cell phones snapping out of focused

    shots of the stunned thirty seven year old with an unmistakable

     bulge. Mr. Land looked down. Sure enough it was there at

    full mast through the hole in his boxers pressed against

     his zipper. Hard.

Mr. Land looked up,

hyperventilated and

balled loudly

letting fat tears splash on his

oblivious erection.

For Love of Rock & Roll

The subwoofer faded out the bassline into a soft pulse.
And then silence. Black lights shined purple stains on Tony's
apartment couch. He waited until the final notes no longer
vibrated, until the CD player glowed the time and number
of tracks on the album in their entirety.
Tony reached for his copy of '1001 Albums to Listen to
Before You Die' and marked off the entry Purple Rain in
red ink. He then pulled out his marble composition
notebook and wrote:
    *"10 out of 10. Prince's the modern virtuoso on par with
any celebrated musical genius from the likes of Mozart to
Michael Jackson."*
Tony shoved the two books underneath the couch
with the dusty pile of other marble notebooks
full of similar short reviews in his handwriting.
'I'm almost there,' he thought.
He was almost to 1001 reviews.
Tony ejected Purple Rain out of the Toshiba player and
              replaced it with the Violent Femmes self-
titled debut.
The unmistakable acoustic bass and snare for the opening
track Blister in the Sun shook the walls of his studio
apartment and he quickly adjusted the levels as
to not disturb his neighbor.
Although the wall served as sufficient soundproofing for
fairly raucous engagements as exhibited by his neighbor's
past drunken blowouts, Tony didn't intend to test the limits of
the foam insulation dividing them.
He toyed with the idea of wearing head phones

from time to time. But the CD player was on the
 other side of the room and he would need to buy
an extension and transformer for the auxiliary jack.
And that would dilute the sound and take away from the
listening experience. He wouldn't be able to give the
albums a fair critique. He could move the couch closer to
the player allowing for headphones to be plugged in directly.
 But that would require him to rearrange all of his furniture,
his coffee table, CD stacks. And worse, it'd require him to
give his one room apartment a much needed cleaning.

It was best that he listen to his albums at a reasonable level
during daylight hours weekday and maybe crank up his sound
system on the weekends.
Tony could probably turn the music up a little
louder during the week. He shared a wall with
only the one neighbor, this young Indian guy.
Although he never complained or pounded on the
wall, Tony didn't want to push his luck.
As Gordon Gado belted out lyrics of adolescent lust
and betrayal over jangly pop melodies, Tony fought the
urge to reach under his couch and mark the Violent Femmes
off his list prematurely. 'No,' he thought. Every album
must be listened to from start to finish. This task wasn't as
 easy as it seemed.
While he neighbor never complained there, were other
factors that could ruin his experience. A solicitor preaching
he word of God could interrupt a song. He kept his phone on
silent, like he would at a movie theater and took other precautions
like turning off the lights and putting towels at the foot of the
doorway
 to give the appearance that no one was home. There were
unexpected
variables that caused him to have to start an album over from time

Once he got a persistent banging at the door
during Elvis Presley is Back! He ignored the
knocking the best he could concentrating on
the soulful voice of the king.
After the album was finished he saw a note was
 shoved under the door through the towel. He read
it and grabbed his phone to make the call.
      "Hey, long time. So when'd dad die?"
Tony asked his sister on the other end of the line.
      "Last night,"
she answered.
      "That's too bad. I'm sorry."
Tony tried to sound sad and even
thought he could force a couple tears. He tried
 to imagine his father's face but could only
picture Elvis's face making his signature lip curl
on the album cover. He went for his 1001 Albums
 to Listen to Before Die book, marked off Elvis
Presley is Back! and wrote in a marble notebook:
      *"7 out of 10. Not the King's best work but even his
weaker efforts are better than the most seasoned rockers'
entire catalogues."*
Tony resolved to answer his door if the knocking
became persistent. He'd give it 30 seconds. 30
seconds of banging would let him know that
it wasn't just some bible thumper or girl
scout. If his mother died it'd be proper to get
 the news from his sister in person.

Tony listened to the Violent Femmes
final track Good Feeling, a slow ballad
 complete with a humble piano
accompaniment and smooth fiddle

solo that melted over the paintbrush
drumsticks on the snare.
Hands on his knees in the dark, he didn't
sway to the music like it begged him to. He
never bobbed his head or tapped his thighs with
 his fingers. He looked forward at the Toshiba CD
player counting down the blue fluorescent
seconds in each track.
 There was a knock at the door.
'Darn it,' he thought. The knock persisted.
 As the song ended Tony got up to answer
to the door. Suddenly, the album's hidden
track 'Ugly' came on just as Tony reached
for the knob. His hand gripped the knob but
he didn't turn. The knocking continued.
Well passed 30 seconds and the hidden track's
 intro, the knocking continued and Joseph stood
anxiety ridden, palm sweating against the knob.
 The knocking got manic, desperate,, two little fist
pounding on the other side.
And then it stopped.
Tony let out an audible sigh and checked
under the door. There was no note.
Thank God. Tony collapsed on his
couch just as the track ended.
He felt a slight rush as he went
for his copy of his 1001 Albums
 to Listen to Before You Die and
marble notebook. He crossed off
Violent Femmes and
made another entry:

"8 out of 10. A remarkable debut and beautiful effort from the trio. Where it lacks in production it more than makes up for in composition and pathos."

Tony ejected the Violent Femmes and

       popped in Def Leppard's Pyromania.

     'I'm almost there,'he thought. The infectious

     guitar lick of 'Rock! Rock!' pounded through

        the Bose speakers and Tony
        decided

          'fuck it,'

     and cranked the sound up.

Perfect

Take a Polaroid picture of God. Shake it and then place
 His image on the copy machine glass face down.
  Be sure to leave dust, streaks, fingerprint smudges,
    stray hairs and other imperfections. Pull the cover over
   sealing the document. Select the desired lightness
      or darkness by pressing a button. Newsprint,
        color to black and white, or photos will need to
         be lightened. Light text, light colors, or pencil drawings
          need to be darkened to show up well. The almighty is
           tricky to capture so try your best to
             highlight the essential qualities.
               Press the large copy button (usually green)
                and wait. When the machine hums and the
                 paper spits out, replace the Polaroid with the
              copy that was just made. Place it face-down
             on the glass and repeat the process.
            When the copy's made replace the copy in
             the machine and make a copy of the copy
             of the original picture. And then make a copy
          of a copy of another copy of the
       original and after that a copy
      of a copy of a copy
      of a copy of
       the
      original.
      Keep repeating
          this process.
            Repeat it for three
                thousand years. Never leave the

same image in the machine.
Notice slight changes the fractured ink,
the breaks in lines. Facial features faded, cracks
from paper folds and warped tints. Vibrant shades of
grey and piercing black blotches from printing malfunctions.
Put in a new ink cartridge to reveal darker features. A slight
mistake in placement on the glass and an arm is lost. Repeat
the process a million times. Make two billion more
copies. Stand in a copy room eyes up, blinded by
four foot flickering fluorescent light tubes behind
acrylic prismatic sheets, lips and nose peering
out of hot Xerox, body buried under
countless reams of life and death.
Savor paper cuts in your neck.
Wriggle free, inch above
your creation.
Wing tips
find
stability
atop compressed
paper piles. Now, search. Dig.
The Polaroid. Dig. Sift through
phonebook thick stacks of documents.
Keep digging. Make your way back towards the
printer. The last place you remember seeing the original
Polaroid. Pay no attention to the images you
crumple and discard to   make a path. Become
frustrated with your efforts. Question genuinely
if there ever was a Polaroid to begin with.
Was there really ever a picture that laid on that
glass that wasn't a copy of some other copy?
Question yourself. Doubt yourself. Concede
defeat   just as you spot it there, right where you left it.
A corner of the Polaroid sticks out like origami.

Grab it. Flip it over. Flatten it. And see yourself. Red eyed and perfect.

9 789388 125994